Special Thanks to Noah Postema and Pearce Brown

To Monica "Mono"

- Jackson Greer

The
Messy
Middle

a poetry collection

for Jared and Mallory

&

for Matthias

Contents

Nor am I the Captain of my Soul, I am only its Noisiest Passenger

We are lonely, but to what are we lonely for?

Did the fig leaves know?

"For I am in a strait betwixt two, having a desire to depart and be with Christ, which is far better."
- Philippians 1:23

Round, Round, Round we go
Worry, Doubt, and Lies in tow
Playing hide & seek with Love
hidden he sits with a look so smug
Drowning in the sea of fate
a soul struggles to find its mate
Our journey is one with a single goal
a heart straining to fill its gaping hole

Sehnsucht's Rapier

....

my foreshadow

longing to long for the feeling again
to know how to know how to be a man

to try to satisfy the insatiable desire
to tame the rage of the consuming fire

blinded by the glaring white light
that comes from the battle with an army of "might"

how to know how to decide of virtues
when the collection of voices provides no clues

Paradise Found

To desire and want
begins a battle already fought
by the greatest of us
those encrusted in rust

A Part of the Whole
each individual role
relies on the rest
to narrowly pass the test

Our teacher grades our work
with a contorted smirk
and decides our grade
based on the standard he's made

Did we meet the goal
or forfeit our soul
in favor of consent
a sum already spent

Sisyphus Exposed

Trapped in the prison of himself
wanting to feel a feeling never felt

Wholly absorbed by his own life
he doesn't see the chains of might

Indulging in desires of the flesh
the chance to escape becomes less and less

Relying on his own power
waiting on that liberating hour

The first generation to see
the world entirely secondhand.
Forgoing the ability to be
a discoverer of new land.

A Representation of the Sacred Well

....

Slowly it falls like blinding rain
seeking to capture and trying to claim
all the temporal success we gain
the money and lies of petty fame
No longer supported by the world's cane
broken we fall, now exposed and lame
succumbing to the harsh nature of the game
reluctantly we release our grip on life's reigns
Rising from addiction to drugs like cocaine
able to see clearly and longing for a new name
yet unaware to the eternal struggle and pain
that comes when you realize nothing will ever be the
same

blank sound

Dwelling in the dread of death
quietly mopping up our untimely mess
A constant buzz drowns out all other sounds
it continues beyond and life and wholly surrounds

Is death simply a hopeless echo
that bounces off walls like a glancing blow?
Do we reach a point of no return
escaping the punishment of fire's burn?

Will we willingly drift into a prolonged sleep
abandoning all material desire to keep?
Or will we proudly cling to our self
reaching for the highest book on the shelf?

Until our time, we continue in fear
unwarranted, unjustified, and imposingly near.

a caged rush

Freely it flowed
for an unmeasured amount of time.
Unable to slow
as it trickled down the line.

Until they decided
to plant a wall of stone.
Suddenly the stream collided
against the rock's rigid bone.

Trapped in a cell
and held captive against its will
with no one to tell
of its desire to fill.

Swirling under the surface
gradually beating against the wall
trying to remember its purpose
and what it was like to fall.

As time goes by
a crack starts to form
and it reaches inside
begging to swarm.

Up the crack reaches
and expands like a web.
Grasping for space, it breaches
and remembers how to ebb.

a potter's mess

these jars of clay
were never meant to stay
put in one place
collecting a dusty face

jagged and shattered
wanting to matter
empty on the inside
longing to imbibe

a benevolent vapour

Through the air it travels
and is swept across the land.
Suspended overhead in clouds
it crafts its plot against man.

When it's finally given the signal
down it falls on its prey.
Unsuspecting victims hardly
realize the sky beginning to gray.

Rooted deep in the skin
it rests and keeps quiet.
Bidding its precious time
letting the body try to fight it.

For some seventy-odd years
the war wages on.
Plagued with ups and downs
and filled with rights and wrongs.

While the sickness spreads its web
and eats away at the heart.
The mind carries on
unaware from the very start.

As the years pass by
and generations are made.
The sickness is quietly passed on
while its power never fades.

And with death comes release
for the first patient zero.
But those left behind
remain in need of a hero.

[But the Savior never came]

They all died sick and waiting
with their hope never dying.
Yet the sickness lingered there
floating in a space still prying.

elevated

Feet slip on the crumbling rock
the wind's howl echoes and mocks

Far down below the water swells
Fear covers the face of the pale

Behind waits a life, unwanted
a heart and mind whose growth is stunted

It only takes one simple step
to fall into a fate never met

Out on the exposed edge
Life waits presenting its pledge

And slowly creeping from underneath
Doubt prepares its commanding leash

The splinters dug into
his now bloody flesh
surrounded he lies in
his own muddy mess

He cries out for help
till his throat becomes raw
desperately waiting to
the see the face of Pa

Why did this happen
he thinks to no one
i should have listened
i knew i was wrong

He closes his eyes
crushed by the world's weight
slowly giving in
to the clutches of fate

a night on the plain

I remember
peering out
behind the flap

Overhead sky
and barren earth
plainly black

god's pencil
drew a flash
across the sky

I heard
my sister
softly cry

Father pulled
me back
inside

Nature's hand
took his
pride

I closed my
eyes and
imagined them

Dipping their
brush to
create again

The beat
of water
brought sleep

Their tears
flowed down
ignoring defeat

Nor am I the Captain of my Soul, I am only its Nosiest Passenger

....

Record of Life

A knock is heard on the door of life
patiently waiting stands an applicant for wife
The lock is turned and in she steps
now faced by a man she didn't expect
Shrouded in a shade and seated across
a table for two she waits with a pause
Compelled to come forward by an unseen force
she slides in her chair to begin the first course
In front of her lays three stacks of paper
one to open now, two others to save for later
She looks toward her host waiting for approval
instead she is met with a look of refusal
Breaking the first seal, she begins to read
unknowingly committing an indelible deed
To her horror she realizes the truth at last
this decayed paper consists of her past
Mouth agape and eyes wide with a look so perplexed
her eyes meet her host's as he whispers, "Next"
Still shocked and reeling she takes the second
slightly curious as to what is the lesson
Turning the pages, she reads a new story
one more familiar a tale of her own glory
The last section fails to lessen the torment
for she has now just read her life to the present
Afraid of the final stack left on the oak
she strains to hear the words the man slowly spoke
"You came here for a reason I do not know why,

have I only this for you," he said with a sigh
The remaining bundle suddenly fell in her lap
strangely eager she pinched the seal with a quick
snap
A look of confusion spread across as her face sank
she turned through the pages to find them all blank

Defeated and Beaten
he opens the door.
The wind blows past
his head with a roar.

She sits at the table
worry on her face.
The candle grows dimmer
as the man starts to pace.

Neither speaks first
for there's nothing to say.
Their eyes downcast
dark like the day.

The wind moans outside
and moves in a swirl.
But they sit silent
deaf to the world.

He throws his pack
and the bottle crawls out.
Her eyes grow wide
with fear and doubt.

He starts to explain
but gives up with a heave.

She starts to sob
and gets up to leave.

In a moment of panic
he grabs her arm.
She twists away
to escape the harm.

But he doesn't let go
his grip only tightens.
She yelps with pain
and continues her fighting.

Then suddenly the room
fills with a snap.
Violently torn her
arm lies limp with a crack.

Stricken with horror
he backs away to flee.
She crumbles to the floor,
exposed, for him to see.

Like a rugged drum
the wind beats on the walls.
In the same moment
a tree swiftly falls.

of a noose

Standing slightly above waiting to be mocked
the crowd below starts to shake the box

Light for a moment, then filling darkness
envelops the world, feeling heartless

Slip it over, nice and crisp
make it quick, there's nothing to risk

Rising throughout the shouts and jeers
ascends the deepest and darkest of fears

Thick and strong, unable to break
it's form-fitted timing is never late

The boards slowly creak and painfully moan
with each ill-fated step under the dome

Unable to see, still straining to hear
wishing again to be desperately near

The floor gives way, gravity does its deed
granting permission to its noblest steed

Stranded there with dangling feet
eternally bound to an unwanted leash

Imagine if Belshezzar and Cortés shared a night

Some don't enjoy the marks of others.
They don't like the scribbled notes and bent covers.
The underlined phrases and torn pages
are like the products of worndown cages.

But some view them as an explorer's map
as a weathered traveller and his eroded packs.
The notes in the margin and trails of ink
make up the well of thoughts from which to drink.

Theodore Dreiser

In his newly pressed suit
he exits the golden door.
Counting his acquired root
and beating back the roar.

Across the covered street
another sits and waits.
Warming his soiled feet
not minding the day's date.

The ironed man trots
snug in his furred coat.
Dusting off the chalk
from what he just wrote.

The other straightens up
his face ready and hopeful.
To see if he's in luck
among all the noble.

His ruby eyes flirt
not wanting to meet the others.
His attention, he must divert
to his more equal brothers.

The lower stretches out
a gnarled frozen paw.
Pleading to end the drought
That's jailed his muzzled maw.

He ignores the icy claw
suspended in his path.
Citing the muddled flaw
grazing below his calf.

The lower retracts his offer
beaten but not defeated.
He knows there will be scoffers
numb to the desire of the cheated.

The heated man continues on
not sparing a minute of time.
When suddenly an idea dawns
what if he eradicated this glaring crime.

Tattered and Torn, lying in a heap
wistfully picturing a better life.
The poor man gets up in a leap
soaring through street like a kite.

Now scorching with urge
and full of desire.
To begin a glorious purge
and light a surging fire.

The beggar, he rises
and sprints down the road.
Brimming with fresh surprises
ignoring the debt he owed.

Ink. Heart.

Holding potential in your hand
the ability to create and plan

Gripping it tightly, pushing down hard
willing into existence, a meager part

Loosely it marks and claws across
an unexplored plain pregnant with loss

And when it runs out the process finally stops
until it is refilled and sent back to the top

There it desperately tries to restart
struggling to return to the lonely heart

It scratches, screams and squeaks
filling valleys and reaching peaks

And when its holder begins to tire
the streaks become finer and finer

Until at last the final wall comes down
trapped in words that don't make a sound

They sat in a row of five
a pair of pink shirts
one solid blue
and two patterned plaid.
They sat rigid like stone
faces permanently molded
into a blank, formal stare
the word, "sir" poised on their lips.
The middle one, the one
with the blue shirt,
wore thick-rimmed glasses
that slightly slid forward with each nod.
Their haircuts were identical
a buzz on the sides
with a little left on the top.
Wrinkles started to form
in the pink's shirt
he leaned back and forth
constantly, as if bowing
to some invisible god.
The one on the end
folded his hands in a way
that looked like hesitant prayer
he shifted and adjusted every
fifteen seconds to try to find
a slightly more comfortable spot.
The one in the pink

had wandering eyes
his gaze lingered one-third
of the way up the woman's body
his shifty eyes scanned
the room, half-daring
anyone to notice him, half-worried
that someone might notice him.
The other plaid shirt
had enormous nostrils
the surrounding air
was no match for his inhale
he took in anything
and everything around his face.
Nearly in unison they turned
their heads to whisper
and make their sarcastic remarks
it was as if they were on a schedule.
An internal clock that
ran the body and
controlled every movement.
One of their watches went
off, making an
announcement only significant
to one.

We are lonely, but to what are we lonely for?

....

Me and You
You and I
destined to last
till the day we die

You and I
Me and You
free at last
but not quite through

Me and You
You and I
lost in love
wanting to survive

You and I
Me and You
running away
still trying to prove

Hearts broken
and love lost
Last words spoken
counting the cost

Of a heart
torn in two
and a remaining part
not quite through

Floating in air
caught in between
the lover's snare
unsure of what it means

Collapsing at the feet
of the unsolved riddle
wanting to repeat
the large and the little

I'd been so used to her right there
a feeling so warm, now cold and bare

What I would give to have you here
standing so close with an open ear

I spend my days turning to see
to be met with the solitude of me

no one there
a hole in the air

Now my words waste away in the wind
and the scars dig deep under the skin

Your absence left more than a gap
a shattered mirror reflecting what I lack

The emptiness of being alone
and the realization of the guilt I own

four a.m.

i still remember the day
in the pouring rain
you were smiling
not minding the pain

i knew in an instant
that i wanted you
and i knew then what
i had to do

Caught up in the distraction of us
everything else held the weight of dust

We were never able to open up
our lives remained two empty cups

You finally revealed your true intentions
but it didn't help our current condition

I knew that I had diagnosed the cancer
I knew that I had found my final answer

a waning love

She placed all her trust in him
and believed him until the very end

They saw the writing upon the wall
a hand shaking and eerily small

Though he mislead
it was she that misread

The words that spelled out something grim
a hopeless, sunless, daybreak dim

She fell and begged at his dusty feet
but only deaf ears did her cries meet

He didn't hear her pleas
and continued to fail to meet her needs.

Touch connects and combines into two
separate parts with only one thing to do.
It creates a longing for purpose and place
and opens up and closes the same space.

But should it be saved for a select few
a sacred bond between only two.
Is it meant to be private and not seen
to leave others guessing and trying to seem.

mine

When the one voice you
hear is only your own
the truth and knowledge
is only available on loan.

an unwanted dwelling

What used to be
we thought it was perfect
Concerned only for 'we'
demands were always met

Focus stayed centered on us
and thoughts weren't allowed to wander
We thought we defeated lust
and had nothing left to conquer

Our eyes stayed locked on each other
absorbed by the magnet of 'love'
Up went our protective cover
and on went the exclusive gloves

Sometimes I wonder about all we missed
the chances and opportunities to serve
Wasting our time trapped in fits
of contrived devotion we thought we deserved

Invitations reluctantly refused
and the people ignored
in favour of fighting to somehow prove
far outnumber the nights on good accord

Regret eats away at my broken heart
not for you, but for the others
The ones I never knew were smart
or the ones I never was allowed to bother

The ones who had a story to tell
and the ones that I never shared a meal with
I want to escape from remorse's cell
and believe that it was all just a myth

But this is how you trained my mind
to ignore and save my attention for you
Deaf to the voice of a different kind
and blind to everything new

So despite all you did
I want to send my thanks
for opening the imaginary lid
of the can holding a second chance

seeking

Touching a heart
and fulfilling desires
Making one feel smart
and reach higher and higher

Its power unmatched
and influence widespread
The ability to go back
And bring life to the dead

interruptions

I close my eyes
to start the act
I think to myself
"what do I say"

How do I address
the one who created me?
How do I talk to
the one who controls me?

[The door opens]

I open my eyes
stopping for a moment
I think to myself
"what do I do"

Do I stop my conversation
with the one above me?
How do I tell
the one who blesses me?

[The door closes]

I close my eyes again
to pick up where I left off
I try to remember
what I was saying

How do I ask
a question never asked?
How do I begin
a process never begun?

[The lights turn off]

I open my eyes again
looking into the darkness
I try to see
what's there, if anything

Do I get up
and see what happened?
Do I wait for
someone else to do something?

[The lights turn on]

I close my eyes
to see if he's still there
I want to know for sure
if someone actually cares

How do I approach
anyone who knows me?
How do I tell them
what is happening?

[The sink drips]

I open my eyes
still straining to see
I want to ignore it
but I can't seem to forget

Do I get up to look
at some other thing?
Do I leave my
place of intimacy for good?

[The sink stops]

I close my eyes, reluctantly
clinging onto the hope
I need to be certain
of what truly matters

How do I let
him know how I feel?
Do I open up
and expose the real me?

[The bed moves]

I open my eyes quickly
my gaze trying to feel
I need to figure out
how to end all of this

Do I leave some
sort of sign?
Do I abandon
the only thing I've known?

[The bed collapses]

Did the fig leaves know?

....

Delirium

Needle, Bottle or Pill
we all seek to fill
the void in this life
and find a fulfilling wife

Too quick to marry
unwilling to carry
the burden on our back
showing what we lack

Our inability to close the hole
highlights the meager role
of our unwanted place
within a forgotten race

So we turn to addiction
continuing the friction
of an inglorious defeat
a fate we are willing to meet

above the veneer

Perched above, muscles tense
scanning ahead, not wanting to miss
anything or anyone
the time has come

Unfurl and uncurl, stretch and reach
grab and take, open up and breach
the barriers before and break through
it's time to get up and try to move

Step and Fall, free for the first
this is what it's like to feel thirst
eyes snap open, the world spins around
as panic takes hold when falling down

Spiraling in a circle, unable to see
dizzy in wonder, raising a plea
for it all to stop and graciously slow
to a capable speed far below

a modern Nebuchadnezzar

Insecurity is our prison
the chains being other's opinions
Hiding behind our vision
adhering to a false religion

Behind a one-way screen
we worship and exalt each other
For the sole purpose to deem
what is worthy among the clutter

We lingered there.
In those extended moments
of five-second connections.
Eyes locked and bodies twisting.
Stares holding and feet jumping.
In that moment nothing mattered.
Our worries and cares retreated.
For a few fleeting seconds
We were surrounded but alone.
As the swarm and thrash
of bodies slithered and flowed
we blended in.

A faint call
a sound small
reaches out
lingers and pouts

Shrill & Clear
simple to hear
then the echo
which far off throws..

an adage: reverse

We give our false approval
wanting to receive it in return
Overseeing the ironic removal
of all we've ever learned

Athanasios

Laughter is the best medicine
and Joy its fellow remedy.
Yet how we encounter each
remains an unsolved mystery.

Masked in curt wit
intellect does its work.
People can't help but
chuckle in controlled spurts.

Or what about one big burst
of uncontained laughter and tears.
With pain in your sides
when remembering the jokes of past years.

It transcends Time and brings us together and
makes us forget worries and hope for the better.

Leftovers

Who understands the world's view of beauty
or the people who think it's their rightful duty
to decide the unwritten, fabricated rules
then subjectively choose from a selective pool

Of older women trying to appear younger
attempting to appease their undying hunger
and adolescent teens trying to seem older
only concerned with culture: the unforgiving beholder

In the end all that remains is money spent
and inflated egos too far gone to relent
The thief of joy is the desire to compare
and its estranged cousin: feelings that don't care

It's too late when the lesson has been learned
the damage has been done and the bridge has been
burned

Obstinate Order

I.

It almost made me
a foolish believer
It almost made me
succumb to the fever

It almost made me
a beggar and poor
It almost made me
a man wanting more

It almost made me
give up in defeat
It almost made me
get up and move my feet

It almost made me
do something I'd regret
It almost made me
place that final bet

II.

It almost made me
talk to that girl
It almost made me
lost in life's swirl

It almost made me
late on that day
It almost made me
unable to really say

It almost made me
free for the first
It almost made me
hunger and thirst

It almost made me
miss the meeting
It almost made me
give up on reading

III.

It almost made me
realize the truth
It almost made me
desert my youth

It almost made me
a catcher in the rye
It almost made me
soar across the sky

It almost made me
write down my thoughts
It almost made me
cast my paltry lot

It almost made me
successful and proud
It almost made me
blindly follow the crowd

IV.

It almost made me
look around the corner
It almost made me
a wandering loner

It almost made me
give up the fight
It almost made me
stay up all night

It almost made me
an uncommitted lover
It almost made me
run for cover

It almost made me
leave my only home
It almost made me
desperately alone

Manufactured by Amazon.com
Columbia, SC
10 April 2017